USC Spouse Petitioning Spouse

How to Petition your Husband or Wife if you are a US Citizen

Attorney Brian D. Lerner

LAW OFFICES OF
BRIAN D. LERNER
A PROFESSIONAL CORPORATION

ATTORNEY DRAFTED IMMIGRATION PETITIONS

By

Brian D. Lerner

Attorney at Law

Disclaimer and Terms of Use:

Effort has been made to ensure that the information in this book is accurate and complete. However, the author and the publisher do not warrant that this particular petition will mirror or be exactly as your situation. There has not been any attorney-client agreement created by the purchase of this petition or application. No legal advice has occurred. The cases, regulations and/or statutes cited may change at any time without notice.

ISBN: 978-1-958990-23-0

INTRODUCTION

There are a multitude of different immigration petitions and applications. They are complex and full of requirements. Obviously, it would be best to hire an immigration attorney to best prepare the petitions and applications. However, this can certainly cost thousands of dollars.

The next best option is to get a sample of the petition written by an experienced immigration attorney. The samples cost a fraction what would be charged by an immigration attorney. However, while the reader has to alter, amend and change the parts of the sample petition to reflect their actual situation, it is a fantastic roadmap for them to use. If the reader has purchased the entire petition or application, they will have real live samples of cover letters, forms, declarations, affidavits and the necessary exhibits to use. The samples come from real cases and the names of those clients have been redacted to protect the privacy of that person or corporation.

These are petitions and applications that have been drafted by an experienced immigration attorney with over 25 years of experience. Get the benefits of that experience without the costs.

CONTENTS

About the Law Offices of Brian D. Lerner

The Law Offices of Brian D. Lerne, APC. The law practice consists of Immigration and Nationality Law and everything involved with and regarding immigration which includes citizenship, investment visas, family and employment visas, removal and deportation hearings, appeals, waivers, adjustment, consulate processing and all types of immigration and citizenship matters. Thousands of families have been reunited and/or permitted to stay in the U.S. and/or return to the U.S. because of the successful work of Immigration Attorney Brian D. Lerner.

This law offices handles all types of immigration cases including family based and employment based. Immigration issues range from immigration court proceedings to trying to fix what paralegals may have done that was neither correct nor proper. Foreign nationals must have experience lawyers admitted to practice law.

The Law Offices of Brian D. Lerner, APC, handles cases arising from business visas, work permits, Green Cards, non-immigrant visas, deportation, citizenship, appeals and all areas of immigration. The Law Offices of Brian D. Lerner, APC does EB-5 Investor Visas, H-1B Specialty Occupation, L-1 Intracompany Transferee, E-2 Treaty Investor, E-1 Treaty Trader, O-1 Extraordinary Ability among others. Regarding immigrant visas for the Green Card, the firm does PERM and advanced degree PERM, Family Petitions, and Extraordinary Alien Petitions. In addition to affirmative petitions, the Law Firm represents people in people in deportation and removal hearings, including political asylum, withholding of removal, and convention against torture cases.

Brian D. Lerner has been certified as an expert in Immigration & Nationality Law by the California State Bar, Board of Legal Specialization since 2000 and has been re-certified three times. He now passes on his decades of experience by allowing the Reader, Law Schools, Professors and other Immigration Attorneys to purchase sample petitions on every facet of Immigration Law.

About the USC Spouse Petitioning Spouse

Ready to Petition your Spouse? In this case, are you a US Citizen and you are petitioning your spouse, it will be considered an Immediate Relative Petition and you can move on immediately (or even simultaneously) to adjusting status or consulate processing. The first part must be done and must be done properly in order to ever proceed to the next part. Without a proper I-130 application there will never be a Green Card. If approved, then you could move onto the next step in the Immigration process. If not approved, it will take years of red tape. Remember, it is your responsibility to submit everything correctly. This sample I-130 Petition has everything necessary to give you the best chance possible to get an approval. Just input your own information and use the application as a guide. It has been prepared by an expert Immigration Attorney. Thus, this book will allow you to see a guide of how it is done, prepared and submitte

ATTORNEY COVER LETTER

Law Offices of Brian D. Lerner

A PROFESSIONAL CORPORATION

CERTIFIED SPECIALIST IN IMMIGRATION AND NATIONALITY LAW
ADMITTED TO THE U.S. SUPREME COURT

LONG BEACH, CALIFORNIA
(562) 495-0554

CARSON, CALIFORNIA
(310) 684-5420

April 9, 2019

U.S. Citizenship and Immigration Services
Attn: I-130
PO Box 21700
Phoenix, AZ 85036

RE: I-130, Petition for Alien Relative
Petitioner: [redacted]
Beneficiary: [redacted]

Dear Sir/Madam:

We hereby submit an I-130, Petition for Alien Relative, for [redacted] (hereinafter "Petitioner') on behalf of her spouse [redacted] (hereinafter "Beneficiary").

Enclosed herein please find the following documents:

FORMS

Form:	**Description:**
G-1145	E-Notification of Application/Petition Acceptance;
G-28	Notice of Entry of Appearance as Attorney or Accredited Representative (Petitioner);
G-28	Notice of Entry of Appearance as Attorney or Accredited Representative (Beneficiary);
I-130	Petition for Alien Relative with $535.00 Filing Fee; and
I-130A	Supplemental Information for Spouse Beneficiary.

We also enclose two passport-style photographs of the Petitioner and Beneficiary.

EXHIBITS

Exhibits:	**Description:**
1.	Petitioner's Birth Certificate;
2.	Petitioner's Passport;

4 Beneficiary's Passport and visa;
5. Petitioner and Beneficiary's Marriage Certificate;
6. Family and Wedding Photos of Petitioner and Beneficiary; and
7. Supporting Letters from the Relatives and Friends of Petitioner and Beneficiary.

Under the Immigration and Nationality Act ("INA") § 201 (b) (2) (A) (i), the Immediate Relatives, including children, spouses and parents of a U.S. citizen may be petitioned for an immigrant visa, without being subjected to direct numerical limitations.

In the present case, the Petitioner is a U.S. citizen. Petitioner and Beneficiary were married on February 28, 2019 in Milton Keynes, Buckinghamshire, United Kingdom. Therefore, Petitioner is qualified to file an Alien Relative Petition on behalf of her spouse, Beneficiary.

Based on the foregoing, we respectfully submit that the attached evidence shows the necessary relationship exists and that the instant I-130 should be approved.

Thank you for your consideration in this matter. Should you have any further questions, please feel free to contact our office at (562) 495-0554.

Sincerely,

Brian D. Lerner
Attorney at Law

FORMS

Notice of Entry of Appearance as Attorney or Accredited Representative

Department of Homeland Security

DHS
Form G-28
OMB No. 1615-0105
Expires 05/31/2021

Part 1. Information About Attorney or Accredited Representative

1. USCIS Online Account Number (if any) ▶

Name of Attorney or Accredited Representative

2.a. Family Name (Last Name) Lerner

2.b. Given Name (First Name) Brian

2.c. Middle Name David

Address of Attorney or Accredited Representative

3.a. Street Number and Name 3233 E Broadway

3.b. ☐ Apt. ☐ Ste. ☐ Flr.

3.c. City or Town Long Beach

3.d. State CA 3.e. ZIP Code 90803

3.f. Province

3.g. Postal Code

3.h. Country
USA

Contact Information of Attorney or Accredited Representative

4. Daytime Telephone Number

5. Mobile Telephone Number (if any)

6. Email Address (if any)
blerner@californiaimmigration.us

7. Fax Number (if any)
(562) 608-8672

Part 2. Eligibility Information for Attorney or Accredited Representative

Select **all applicable** items.

1.a. ☒ I am an attorney eligible to practice law in, and a member in good standing of, the bar of the highest courts of the following states, possessions, territories, commonwealths, or the District of Columbia. If you need extra space to complete this section, use the space provided in **Part 6. Additional Information.**

Licensing Authority
Supreme Court of California

1.b. Bar Number (if applicable)

1.c. I (select **only one** box) ☒ am not ☐ am subject to any order suspending, enjoining, restraining, disbarring, or otherwise restricting me in the practice of law. If you are subject to any orders, use the space provided in **Part 6. Additional Information** to provide an explanation.

1.d. Name of Law Firm or Organization (if applicable)
Law Offices of Brian D Lerner

2.a. ☐ I am an accredited representative of the following qualified nonprofit religious, charitable, social service, or similar organization established in the United States and recognized by the Department of Justice in accordance with 8 CFR part 1292.

2.b. Name of Recognized Organization

2.c. Date of Accreditation (mm/dd/yyyy)

3. ☐ I am associated with ______, the attorney or accredited representative of record who previously filed Form G-28 in this case, and my appearance as an attorney or accredited representative for a limited purpose is at his or her request.

4.a. ☐ I am a law student or law graduate working under the direct supervision of the attorney or accredited representative of record on this form in accordance with the requirements in 8 CFR 292.1(a)(2).

4.b. Name of Law Student or Law Graduate

Part 3. Notice of Appearance as Attorney or Accredited Representative

If you need extra space to complete this section, use the space provided in **Part 6. Additional Information**.

This appearance relates to immigration matters before (select **only one** box):

1.a. [X] U.S. Citizenship and Immigration Services (USCIS)

1.b. List the form numbers or specific matter in which appearance is entered.

I-130

2.a. [ ] U.S. Immigration and Customs Enforcement (ICE)

2.b. List the specific matter in which appearance is entered.

3.a. [ ] U.S. Customs and Border Protection (CBP)

3.b. List the specific matter in which appearance is entered.

4. Receipt Number (if any)

▶

5. I enter my appearance as an attorney or accredited representative at the request of the (select **only one** box):

[ ] Applicant [X] Petitioner [ ] Requestor
[ ] Beneficiary/Derivative [ ] Respondent (ICE, CBP)

Information About Client (Applicant, Petitioner, Requestor, Beneficiary or Derivative, Respondent, or Authorized Signatory for an Entity)

6.a. Family Name (Last Name) [redacted]

6.b. Given Name (First Name) [redacted]

6.c. Middle Name Nicole

7.a. Name of Entity (if applicable)

7.b. Title of Authorized Signatory for Entity (if applicable)

8. Client's USCIS Online Account Number (if any)

▶

9. Client's Alien Registration Number (A-Number) (if any)

▶ A-

Client's Contact Information

10. Daytime Telephone Number

11. Mobile Telephone Number (if any)

12. Email Address (if any)

[redacted]gmail.com

Mailing Address of Client

NOTE: Provide the client's mailing address. **Do not** provide the business mailing address of the attorney or accredited representative **unless** it serves as the safe mailing address on the application or petition being filed with this Form G-28.

13.a. Street Number and Name [redacted]

13.b. [X] Apt. [ ] Ste. [ ] Flr. E

13.c. City or Town Long Beach

13.d. State CA 13.e. ZIP Code 90802

13.f. Province

13.g. Postal Code

13.h. Country

USA

Part 4. Client's Consent to Representation and Signature

Consent to Representation and Release of Information

I have requested the representation of and consented to being represented by the attorney or accredited representative named in **Part 1.** of this form. According to the Privacy Act of 1974 and U.S. Department of Homeland Security (DHS) policy, I also consent to the disclosure to the named attorney or accredited representative of any records pertaining to me that appear in any system of records of USCIS, ICE, or CBP.

Part 4. Client's Consent to Representation and Signature (continued)

Options Regarding Receipt of USCIS Notices and Documents

USCIS will send notices to both a represented party (the client) and his, her, or its attorney or accredited representative either through mail or electronic delivery. USCIS will send all secure identity documents and Travel Documents to the client's U.S. mailing address.

If you want to have notices and/or secure identity documents sent to your attorney or accredited representative of record rather than to you, please select **all applicable** items below. You may change these elections through written notice to USCIS.

1.a. [X] I request that USCIS send original notices on an application or petition to the business address of my attorney or accredited representative as listed in this form.

1.b. [ ] I request that USCIS send any secure identity document (Permanent Resident Card, Employment Authorization Document, or Travel Document) that I receive to the U.S. business address of my attorney or accredited representative (or to a designated military or diplomatic address in a foreign country (if permitted)).

NOTE: If your notice contains Form I-94, Arrival-Departure Record, USCIS will send the notice to the U.S. business address of your attorney or accredited representative. If you would rather have your Form I-94 sent directly to you, select **Item Number 1.c.**

1.c. [ ] I request that USCIS send my notice containing Form I-94 to me at my U.S. mailing address.

Signature of Client or Authorized Signatory for an Entity

2.a. Signature of Client or Authorized Signatory for an Entity

2.b. Date of Signature (mm/dd/yyyy) 4-4-19

Part 5. Signature of Attorney or Accredited Representative

I have read and understand the regulations and conditions contained in 8 CFR 103.2 and 292 governing appearances and representation before DHS. I declare under penalty of perjury under the laws of the United States that the information I have provided on this form is true and correct.

1. a. Signature of Attorney or Accredited Representative

1.b. Date of Signature (mm/dd/yyyy)

2.a. Signature of Law Student or Law Graduate

2.b. Date of Signature (mm/dd/yyyy)

Part 6. Additional Information

If you need extra space to provide any additional information within this form, use the space below. If you need more space than what is provided, you may make copies of this page to complete and file with this form or attach a separate sheet of paper. Type or print your name at the top of each sheet; indicate the **Page Number, Part Number,** and **Item Number** to which your answer refers; and sign and date each sheet.

1.a Family Name (Last Name) [redacted]

1.b. Given Name (First Name) [redacted]

1.c. Middle Name [redacted]

2.a. Page Number 2.b. Part Number 2.c. Item Number

2.d.

3.a. Page Number 3.b. Part Number 3.c. Item Number

3.d.

4.a. Page Number 4.b. Part Number 4.c. Item Number

4.d.

5.a. Page Number 5.b. Part Number 5.c. Item Number

5.d.

6.a. Page Number 6.b. Part Number 6.c. Item Number

6.d.

Notice of Entry of Appearance as Attorney or Accredited Representative

Department of Homeland Security

DHS
Form G-28
OMB No. 1615-0105
Expires 05/31/2021

Part 1. Information About Attorney or Accredited Representative

1. USCIS Online Account Number (if any) ▶

Name of Attorney or Accredited Representative

2.a. Family Name (Last Name) Lerner

2.b. Given Name (First Name) Brian

2.c. Middle Name David

Address of Attorney or Accredited Representative

3.a. Street Number and Name 3233 E Broadway

3.b. ☐ Apt. ☐ Ste. ☐ Flr.

3.c. City or Town Long Beach

3.d. State CA 3.e. ZIP Code 90803

3.f. Province

3.g. Postal Code

3.h. Country USA

Contact Information of Attorney or Accredited Representative

4. Daytime Telephone Number (562) 495-0554

5. Mobile Telephone Number (if any)

6. Email Address (if any) blerner@californiaimmigration.us

7. Fax Number (if any) (562) 608-8672

Part 2. Eligibility Information for Attorney or Accredited Representative

Select all applicable items.

1.a. ☒ I am an attorney eligible to practice law in, and a member in good standing of, the bar of the highest courts of the following states, possessions, territories, commonwealths, or the District of Columbia. If you need extra space to complete this section, use the space provided in **Part 6. Additional Information.**

Licensing Authority Supreme Court of Califomia

1.b. Bar Number (if applicable)

1.c. I (select only one box) ☒ am not ☐ am subject to any order suspending, enjoining, restraining, disbarring, or otherwise restricting me in the practice of law. If you are subject to any orders, use the space provided in **Part 6. Additional Information** to provide an explanation.

1.d. Name of Law Firm or Organization (if applicable) Law Offices of Brian D Lerner

2.a. ☐ I am an accredited representative of the following qualified nonprofit religious, charitable, social service, or similar organization established in the United States and recognized by the Department of Justice in accordance with 8 CFR part 1292.

2.b. Name of Recognized Organization

2.c. Date of Accreditation (mm/dd/yyyy)

3. ☐ I am associated with ________, the attorney or accredited representative of record who previously filed Form G-28 in this case, and my appearance as an attorney or accredited representative for a limited purpose is at his or her request.

4.a. ☐ I am a law student or law graduate working under the direct supervision of the attorney or accredited representative of record on this form in accordance with the requirements in 8 CFR 292.1(a)(2).

4.b. Name of Law Student or Law Graduate

Part 3. Notice of Appearance as Attorney or Accredited Representative

If you need extra space to complete this section, use the space provided in **Part 6. Additional Information.**

This appearance relates to immigration matters before (select **only one** box):

1.a. ☒ U.S. Citizenship and Immigration Services (USCIS)

1.b. List the form numbers or specific matter in which appearance is entered.

I-130A

2.a. ☐ U.S. Immigration and Customs Enforcement (ICE)

2.b. List the specific matter in which appearance is entered.

3.a. ☐ U.S. Customs and Border Protection (CBP)

3.b. List the specific matter in which appearance is entered.

4. Receipt Number (if any)

▶

5. I enter my appearance as an attorney or accredited representative at the request of the (select **only one** box):

☒ Applicant ☐ Petitioner ☐ Requestor
☐ Beneficiary/Derivative ☐ Respondent (ICE, CBP)

Information About Client (Applicant, Petitioner, Requestor, Beneficiary or Derivative, Respondent, or Authorized Signatory for an Entity)

6.a. Family Name (Last Name)

6.b. Given Name (First Name)

6.c. Middle Name

7.a. Name of Entity (if applicable)

7.b. Title of Authorized Signatory for Entity (if applicable)

8. Client's USCIS Online Account Number (if any)

▶

9. Client's Alien Registration Number (A-Number) (if any)

▶ A-

Client's Contact Information

10. Daytime Telephone Number

11. Mobile Telephone Number (if any)

12. Email Address (if any)

Mailing Address of Client

NOTE: Provide the client's mailing address. **Do not** provide the business mailing address of the attorney or accredited representative **unless** it serves as the safe mailing address on the application or petition being filed with this Form G-28.

13.a. Street Number and Name

13.b. ☒ Apt. ☐ Ste. ☐ Flr.

13.c. City or Town Long Beach

13.d. State CA **13.e.** ZIP Code

13.f. Province

13.g. Postal Code

13.h. Country

USA

Part 4. Client's Consent to Representation and Signature

Consent to Representation and Release of Information

I have requested the representation of and consented to being represented by the attorney or accredited representative named in **Part 1.** of this form. According to the Privacy Act of 1974 and U.S. Department of Homeland Security (DHS) policy, I also consent to the disclosure to the named attorney or accredited representative of any records pertaining to me that appear in any system of records of USCIS, ICE, or CBP.

Part 4. Client's Consent to Representation and Signature (continued)

Options Regarding Receipt of USCIS Notices and Documents

USCIS will send notices to both a represented party (the client) and his, her, or its attorney or accredited representative either through mail or electronic delivery. USCIS will send all secure identity documents and Travel Documents to the client's U.S. mailing address.

If you want to have notices and/or secure identity documents sent to your attorney or accredited representative of record rather than to you, please select **all applicable** items below. You may change these elections through written notice to USCIS.

1.a. [X] I request that USCIS send original notices on an application or petition to the business address of my attorney or accredited representative as listed in this form.

1.b. [ ] I request that USCIS send any secure identity document (Permanent Resident Card, Employment Authorization Document, or Travel Document) that I receive to the U.S. business address of my attorney or accredited representative (or to a designated military or diplomatic address in a foreign country (if permitted)).

NOTE: If your notice contains Form I-94, Arrival-Departure Record, USCIS will send the notice to the U.S. business address of your attorney or accredited representative. If you would rather have your Form I-94 sent directly to you, select **Item Number 1.c.**

1.c. [ ] I request that USCIS send my notice containing Form I-94 to me at my U.S. mailing address.

Signature of Client or Authorized Signatory for an Entity

2.a. Signature of Client or Authorized Signatory for an Entity

[signature]

2.b. Date of Signature (mm/dd/yyyy) 03/24/2015

Part 5. Signature of Attorney or Accredited Representative

I have read and understand the regulations and conditions contained in 8 CFR 103.2 and 292 governing appearances and representation before DHS. I declare under penalty of perjury under the laws of the United States that the information I have provided on this form is true and correct.

1.a. Signature of Attorney or Accredited Representative

[signature]

1.b. Date of Signature (mm/dd/yyyy)

2.a. Signature of Law Student or Law Graduate

2.b. Date of Signature (mm/dd/yyyy)

Part 6. Additional Information

If you need extra space to provide any additional information within this form, use the space below. If you need more space than what is provided, you may make copies of this page to complete and file with this form or attach a separate sheet of paper. Type or print your name at the top of each sheet; indicate the **Page Number, Part Number, and Item Number** to which your answer refers; and sign and date each sheet.

1.a Family Name (Last Name) [redacted]

1.b. Given Name (First Name) [redacted]

1.c. Middle Name Thomas

2.a. Page Number 2.b. Part Number 2.c. Item Number

2.d.

3.a. Page Number 3.b. Part Number 3.c. Item Number

3.d.

4.a. Page Number 4.b. Part Number 4.c. Item Number

4.d.

5.a. Page Number 5.b. Part Number 5.c. Item Number

5.d.

6.a. Page Number 6.b. Part Number 6.c. Item Number

6.d.

Petition for Alien Relative

Department of Homeland Security
U.S. Citizenship and Immigration Services

USCIS
Form I-130
OMB No. 1615-0012
Expires 07/31/2018

For USCIS Use Only	Fee Stamp	Action Stamp
A-Number A-		
Initial Receipt		
Resubmitted		

Relocated	Section of Law/Visa Category		
Received	☐ 201(b) Spouse - IR-1/CR-1	☐ 203(a)(1) Unm. S/D - F1-1	☐ 203(a)(2)(B) Unm. S/D - F2-4
Sent	☐ 201(b) Child - IR-2/CR-2	☐ 203(a)(2)(A) Spouse - F2-1	☐ 203(a)(3) Married S/D - F3-1
Completed	☐ 201(b) Parent - IR-5	☐ 203(a)(2)(A) Child - F2-2	☐ 203(a)(4) Brother/Sister - F4-1

Approved	Petition was filed on (Priority Date mm/dd/yyyy)	☐ Field Investigation	☐ Personal Interview	☐ 204(a)(2)(A) Resolved
Returned	PDR request granted/denied - New priority date (mm/dd/yyyy)	☐ Previously Forwarded	☐ Pet. A-File Reviewed	☐ I-485 Filed Simultaneously
		☐ 203(g) Resolved	☐ Ben. A-File Reviewed	☐ 204(g) Resolved
Remarks				

At which USCIS office (e.g., NBC, VSC, LOS, CRO) was Form I-130 adjudicated? ____________

To be completed by an attorney or accredited representative (if any).

☒ Select this box if Form G-28 is attached.	Volag Number (if any)	Attorney State Bar Number (if applicable)	Attorney or Accredited Representative USCIS Online Account Number (if any)
		[redacted]	

► **START HERE - Type or print in black ink.**

If you need extra space to complete any section of this petition, use the space provided in **Part 9. Additional Information. Complete and submit as many copies of Part 9., as necessary, with your petition.**

Part 1. Relationship (You are the Petitioner. Your relative is the Beneficiary)

1. I am filing this petition for my (Select **only one** box):
   ☒ Spouse ☐ Parent ☐ Brother/Sister ☐ Child
2. If you are filing this petition for your child or parent, select the box that describes your relationship (Select **only one** box):
   ☐ Child was born to parents who were married to each other at the time of the child's birth
   ☐ Stepchild/Stepparent
   ☐ Child was born to parents who were not married to each other at the time of the child's birth
   ☐ Child was adopted (not an Orphan or Hague Convention adoptee)
3. If the beneficiary is your brother/sister, are you related by adoption? ☐ Yes ☒ No
4. Did you gain lawful permanent resident status or citizenship through adoption? ☐ Yes ☒ No

Part 2. Information About You (Petitioner)

1. Alien Registration Number (A-Number) (if any)
   ► A-
2. USCIS Online Account Number (if any)
   ►
3. U.S. Social Security Number (if any)
   ► [redacted]

Your Full Name

4.a. Family Name (Last Name) [redacted]
4.b. Given Name (First Name) [redacted]
4.c. Middle Name [redacted]

Part 2. Information About You (Petitioner) (continued)

Other Names Used (if any)

Provide all other names you have ever used, including aliases, maiden name, and nicknames.

5.a. Family Name (Last Name) None

5.b. Given Name (First Name)

5.c. Middle Name

Other Information

6. City/Town/Village of Birth
Whittier

7. Country of Birth
USA

8. Date of Birth (mm/dd/yyyy) 05/21/1990

9. Sex ☐ Male ☒ Female

Mailing Address

10.a. In Care Of Name

10.b. Street Number and Name

10.c. ☒ Apt. ☐ Ste. ☐ Flr.

10.d. City or Town Long Beach

10.e. State CA 10.f. ZIP Code 90802

10.g. Province

10.h. Postal Code

10.i. Country
USA

11. Is your current mailing address the same as your physical address? ☒ Yes ☐ No

If you answered "No" to **Item Number 11.**, provide information on your physical address in **Item Numbers 12.a. - 13.b.**

Address History

Provide your physical addresses for the last five years, whether inside or outside the United States. Provide your current address first if it is different from your mailing address in **Item Numbers 10.a. - 10.i.**

Physical Address 1

12.a. Street Number and Name

12.b. ☐ Apt. ☐ Ste. ☐ Flr.

12.c. City or Town

12.d. State 12.e. ZIP Code

12.f. Province

12.g. Postal Code

12.h. Country

13.a. Date From (mm/dd/yyyy)

13.b. Date To (mm/dd/yyyy)

Physical Address 2

14.a. Street Number and Name

14.b. ☒ Apt. ☐ Ste. ☐ Flr.

14.c. City or Town Long Beach

14.d. State CA 14.e. ZIP Code

14.f. Province

14.g. Postal Code

14.h. Country
USA

15.a. Date From (mm/dd/yyyy) 11/01/2015

15.b. Date To (mm/dd/yyyy) 05/25/2016

Your Marital Information

16. How many times have you been married? ▶ 1

17. Current Marital Status

☐ Single, Never Married ☒ Married ☐ Divorced
☐ Widowed ☐ Separated ☐ Annulled

Part 2. Information About You (Petitioner) (continued)

18. Date of Current Marriage (if currently married) (mm/dd/yyyy) 02/28./2019

Place of Your Current Marriage (if married)

19.a. City or Town

19.b. State

19.c. Province

19.d. Country

Names of All Your Spouses (if any)

Provide information on your current spouse (if currently married) first and then list all your prior spouses (if any).

Spouse 1

20.a. Family Name (Last Name)

20.b. Given Name (First Name)

20.c. Middle Name Thomas

21. Date Marriage Ended (mm/dd/yyyy)

Spouse 2

22.a. Family Name (Last Name)

22.b. Given Name (First Name)

22.c. Middle Name

23. Date Marriage Ended (mm/dd/yyyy)

Information About Your Parents

Parent 1's Information

Full Name of Parent 1

24.a. Family Name (Last Name)

24.b. Given Name (First Name) Thomas

24.c. Middle Name Brian

25. Date of Birth (mm/dd/yyyy) 01/05/1965

26. Sex ☒ Male ☐ Female

27. Country of Birth

28. City/Town/Village of Residence

29. Country of Residence

Parent 2's Information

Full Name of Parent 2

30.a. Family Name (Last Name)

30.b. Given Name (First Name)

30.c. Middle Name

31. Date of Birth (mm/dd/yyyy) 12/27/1965

32. Sex ☐ Male ☒ Female

33. Country of Birth USA

34. City/Town/Village of Residence Oceanside

35. Country of Residence USA

Additional Information About You (Petitioner)

36. I am a (Select only one box): ☒ U.S. Citizen ☐ Lawful Permanent Resident

If you are a U.S. citizen, complete Item Number 37.

37. My citizenship was acquired through (Select only one box):

☒ Birth in the United States

☐ Naturalization

☐ Parents

38. Have you obtained a Certificate of Naturalization or a Certificate of Citizenship? ☐ Yes ☒ No

If you answered "Yes" to **Item Number 38.**, complete the following:

39.a. Certificate Number

39.b. Place of Issuance

39.c. Date of Issuance (mm/dd/yyyy)

Part 2. Information About You (Petitioner) (continued)

If you are a lawful permanent resident, complete **Item Numbers 40.a. - 41.**

40.a. Class of Admission

40.b. Date of Admission (mm/dd/yyyy)

Place of Admission

40.c. City or Town

40.d State

41. Did you gain lawful permanent resident status through marriage to a U.S. citizen or lawful permanent resident?

☐ Yes ☐ No

Employment History

Provide your employment history for the last five years, whether inside or outside the United States. Provide your current employment first. If you are currently unemployed, type or print "Unemployed" in **Item Number 42.**

Employer 1

42. Name of Employer/Company [redacted]

43.a. Street Number and Name [redacted]

43.b. ☐ Apt. ☐ Ste. ☐ Flr.

43.c. City or Town Long Beach

43.d. State CA **43.e.** ZIP Code [redacted]

43.f. Province

43.g. Postal Code

43.h. Country USA

44. Your Occupation Crematory Supervisor

45.a. Date From (mm/dd/yyyy) 01/18/2015

45.b. Date To (mm/dd/yyyy) PRESENT

Employer 2

46. Name of Employer/Company [redacted]

47.a. Street Number and Name [redacted]

47.b. ☐ Apt. ☐ Ste. ☐ Flr.

47.c. City or Town [redacted]

47.d. State CA **47.e.** ZIP Code [redacted]

47.f. Province

47.g. Postal Code

47.h. Country USA

48. Your Occupation Funeral Assistant

49.a. Date From (mm/dd/yyyy) 07/04/2014

49.b. Date To (mm/dd/yyyy) 12/05/2014

Part 3. Biographic Information

NOTE: Provide the biographic information about you, the petitioner.

1. Ethnicity (Select **only one** box)

☐ Hispanic or Latino
☒ Not Hispanic or Latino

2. Race (Select **all applicable** boxes)

☒ White
☐ Asian
☐ Black or African American
☐ American Indian or Alaska Native
☐ Native Hawaiian or Other Pacific Islander

3. Height Feet 5 Inches 9

4. Weight Pounds 1 5 5

5. Eye Color (Select **only one** box)

☐ Black ☐ Blue ☐ Brown
☐ Gray ☐ Green ☒ Hazel
☐ Maroon ☐ Pink ☐ Unknown/Other

Part 3. Biographic Information (continued)

6. Hair Color (Select only one box)

☐ Bald (No hair) ☒ Black ☐ Blond
☐ Brown ☐ Gray ☐ Red
☐ Sandy ☐ White ☐ Unknown/Other

Part 4. Information About Beneficiary

1. Alien Registration Number (A-Number) (if any)
▶ A-

2. USCIS Online Account Number (if any)
▶

3. U.S. Social Security Number (if any)
▶

Beneficiary's Full Name

4.a. Family Name (Last Name)

4.b. Given Name (First Name)

4.c. Middle Name

Other Names Used (if any)

Provide all other names the beneficiary has ever used, including aliases, maiden name, and nicknames.

5.a. Family Name (Last Name)

5.b. Given Name (First Name)

5.c. Middle Name

Other Information About Beneficiary

6. City/Town/Village of Birth

7. Country of Birth

8. Date of Birth (mm/dd/yyyy) 07/12/1982

9. Sex ☒ Male ☐ Female

10. Has anyone else ever filed a petition for the beneficiary?
☐ Yes ☒ No ☐ Unknown

NOTE: Select "Unknown" *only* if you do not know, and the beneficiary also does not know, if anyone else has ever filed a petition for the beneficiary.

Beneficiary's Physical Address

If the beneficiary lives outside the United States in a home without a street number or name, leave **Item Numbers 11.a.** and **11.b.** blank.

11.a. Street Number and Name

11.b. ☒ Apt. ☐ Ste. ☐ Flr. D

11.c. City or Town

11.d. State 11.e. ZIP Code

11.f. Province

11.g. Postal Code

11.h. Country

Other Address and Contact Information

Provide the address in the United States where the beneficiary intends to live, if different from **Item Numbers 11.a. - 11.h.** If the address is the same, type or print "SAME" in **Item Number 12.a.**

12.a Street Number and Name

12.b. ☒ Apt. ☐ Ste. ☐ Flr.

12.c. City or Town Long Beach

12.d. State CA 12.e. ZIP Code

Provide the beneficiary's address outside the United States, if different from **Item Numbers 11.a. - 11.h.** If the address is the same, type or print "SAME" in **Item Number 13.a.**

13.a. Street Number and Name SAME

13.b. ☐ Apt. ☐ Ste. ☐ Flr.

13.c. City or Town

13.d. Province

13.e. Postal Code

13.f. Country

14. Daytime Telephone Number (if any)

Part 4. Information About Beneficiary (continued)

15. Mobile Telephone Number (if any) [redacted]

16. Email Address (if any) [redacted]

Beneficiary's Marital Information

17. How many times has the beneficiary been married? ▶ 1

18. Current Marital Status

☐ Single, Never Married ☒ Married ☐ Divorced

☐ Widowed ☐ Separated ☐ Annulled

19. Date of Current Marriage (if currently married) (mm/dd/yyyy) 02/28/2019

Place of Beneficiary's Current Marriage (if married)

20.a. City or Town [redacted]

20.b. State

20.c. Province [redacted]

20.d. Country [redacted]

Names of Beneficiary's Spouses (if any)

Provide information on the beneficiary's current spouse (if currently married) first and then list all the beneficiary's prior spouses (if any).

Spouse 1

21.a. Family Name (Last Name) [redacted]

21.b. Given Name (First Name) [redacted]

21.c. Middle Name [redacted]

22. Date Marriage Ended (mm/dd/yyyy)

Spouse 2

23.a. Family Name (Last Name)

23.b. Given Name (First Name)

23.c. Middle Name

24. Date Marriage Ended (mm/dd/yyyy)

Information About Beneficiary's Family

Provide information about the beneficiary's spouse and children.

Person 1

25.a. Family Name (Last Name) [redacted]

25.b. Given Name (First Name) [redacted]

25.c. Middle Name [redacted]

26. Relationship Spouse

27. Date of Birth (mm/dd/yyyy) 05/21/1990

28. Country of Birth USA

Person 2

29.a. Family Name (Last Name)

29.b. Given Name (First Name)

29.c. Middle Name

30. Relationship

31. Date of Birth (mm/dd/yyyy)

32. Country of Birth

Person 3

33.a. Family Name (Last Name)

33.b. Given Name (First Name)

33.c. Middle Name

34. Relationship

35. Date of Birth (mm/dd/yyyy)

36. Country of Birth

Part 4. Information About Beneficiary (continued)

Person 4

37.a. Family Name (Last Name)

37.b. Given Name (First Name)

37.c. Middle Name

38. Relationship

39. Date of Birth (mm/dd/yyyy)

40. Country of Birth

Person 5

41.a. Family Name (Last Name)

41.b. Given Name (First Name)

41.c. Middle Name

42. Relationship

43. Date of Birth (mm/dd/yyyy)

44. Country of Birth

Beneficiary's Entry Information

45. Was the beneficiary EVER in the United States?

☒ Yes ☐ No

If the beneficiary is currently in the United States, complete **Items Numbers 46.a. - 46.d.**

46.a. He or she arrived as a (Class of Admission):

Visitor

46.b. Form I-94 Arrival-Departure Record Number

► N / A

46.c. Date of Arrival (mm/dd/yyyy) 12/26/2018

46.d. Date authorized stay expired, or will expire, as shown on Form I-94 or Form I-95 (mm/dd/yyyy) or type or print "D/S" for Duration of Status

N/A

47. Passport Number

48. Travel Document Number

49. Country of Issuance for Passport or Travel Document

50. Expiration Date for Passport or Travel Document (mm/dd/yyyy) 05/07/2020

Beneficiary's Employment Information

Provide the beneficiary's current employment information (if applicable), even if they are employed outside of the United States. If the beneficiary is currently unemployed, type or print "Unemployed" in **Item Number 51.a.**

51.a. Name of Current Employer (if applicable)

RJC Projects Engineering LTD

51.b. Street Number and Name

51.c. ☐ Apt. ☐ Ste. ☐ Flr.

51.d. City or Town

51.e. State

51.f. ZIP Code

51.g. Province

51.h. Postal Code

51.i. Country

52. Date Employment Began (mm/dd/yyyy) 08/0 1/2008

Additional Information About Beneficiary

53. Was the beneficiary EVER in immigration proceedings?

☐ Yes ☒ No

54. If you answered "Yes," select the type of proceedings and provide the location and date of the proceedings.

☐ Removal ☐ Exclusion/Deportation

☐ Rescission ☐ Other Judicial Proceedings

55.a. City or Town

55.b. State

56. Date (mm/dd/yyyy)

Part 4. Information About Beneficiary (continued)

If the beneficiary's native written language does not use Roman letters, type or print his or her name and foreign address in their native written language.

57.a. Family Name (Last Name)

57.b. Given Name (First Name)

57.c. Middle Name

58.a. Street Number and Name

58.b. ☐ Apt. ☐ Ste. ☐ Flr.

58.c. City or Town

58.d. Province

58.e. Postal Code

58.f. Country

If filing for your spouse, provide the last address at which you physically lived together. If you never lived together, type or print, "Never lived together" in Item Number 59.a.

59.a. Street Number and Name [redacted]

59.b. ☒ Apt. ☐ Ste [redacted]

59.c. City or Town [redacted]

59.d. State 59.e. ZIP Code

59.f. Province [redacted]

59.g. Postal Code [redacted]

59.h. Country
United Kingdom

60.a. Date From (mm/dd/yyyy) 11/2018

60.b. Date To (mm/dd/yyyy) 02/2019

The beneficiary is in the United States and will apply for adjustment of status to that of a lawful permanent resident at the U.S. Citizenship and Immigration Services (USCIS) office in:

61.a. City or Town

61.b. State

The beneficiary will not apply for adjustment of status in the United States, but he or she will apply for an immigrant visa abroad at the U.S. Embassy or U.S. Consulate in:

62.a. City or Town London

62.b. Province

62.c. Country

NOTE: Choosing a U.S. Embassy or U.S. Consulate outside the country of the beneficiary's last residence does not guarantee that it will accept the beneficiary's case for processing. In these situations, the designated U.S. Embassy or U.S. Consulate has discretion over whether or not to accept the beneficiary's case.

Part 5. Other Information

1. Have you EVER previously filed a petition for this beneficiary or any other alien? ☐ Yes ☐ No

If you answered "Yes," provide the name, place, date of filing, and the result.

2.a. Family Name (Last Name)

2.b. Given Name (First Name)

2.c. Middle Name

3.a. City or Town

3.b. State

4. Date Filed (mm/dd/yyyy)

5. Result (for example, approved, denied, withdrawn)

If you are also submitting separate petitions for other relatives, provide the names of and your relationship to each relative.

Relative 1

6.a. Family Name (Last Name)

6.b. Given Name (First Name)

6.c. Middle Name

7. Relationship

Part 5. Other Information (continued)

Relative 2

8.a. Family Name (Last Name)

8.b. Given Name (First Name)

8.c. Middle Name

9. Relationship

WARNING: USCIS investigates the claimed relationships and verifies the validity of documents you submit. If you falsify a family relationship to obtain a visa, USCIS may seek to have you criminally prosecuted.

PENALTIES: By law, you may be imprisoned for up to 5 years or fined $250,000, or both, for entering into a marriage contract in order to evade any U.S. immigration law. In addition, you may be fined up to $10,000 and imprisoned for up to 5 years, or both, for knowingly and willfully falsifying or concealing a material fact or using any false document in submitting this petition.

Part 6. Petitioner's Statement, Contact Information, Declaration, and Signature

NOTE: Read the **Penalties** section of the Form I-130 Instructions before completing this part.

Petitioner's Statement

NOTE: Select the box for either **Item Number 1.a.** or **1.b.** If applicable, select the box for **Item Number 2.**

1.a. [X] I can read and understand English, and I have read and understand every question and instruction on this petition and my answer to every question.

1.b. [ ] The interpreter named in **Part 7.** read to me every question and instruction on this petition and my answer to every question in

a language in which I am fluent. I understood all of this information as interpreted.

2. [X] At my request, the preparer named in **Part 8.**,

Bri an D. Lerner

prepared this petition for me based only upon information I provided or authorized.

Petitioner's Contact Information

3. Petitioner's Daytime Telephone Number

4. Petitioner's Mobile Telephone Number (if any)

5. Petitioner's Email Address (if any)

g t@gmai l.com

Petitioner's Declaration and Certification

Copies of any documents I have submitted are exact photocopies of unaltered, original documents, and I understand that USCIS may require that I submit original documents to USCIS at a later date. Furthermore, I authorize the release of any information from any of my records that USCIS may need to determine my eligibility for the immigration benefit I seek.

I further authorize release of information contained in this petition, in supporting documents, and in my USCIS records to other entities and persons where necessary for the administration and enforcement of U.S. immigration laws.

I understand that USCIS may require me to appear for an appointment to take my biometrics (fingerprints, photograph, and/or signature) and, at that time, if I am required to provide biometrics, I will be required to sign an oath reaffirming that:

1) I provided or authorized all of the information contained in, and submitted with, my petition;

2) I reviewed and understood all of the information in, and submitted with, my petition; and

3) All of this information was complete, true, and correct at the time of filing.

I certify, under penalty of perjury, that all of the information in my petition and any document submitted with it were provided or authorized by me, that I reviewed and understand all of the information contained in, and submitted with, my petition, and that all of this information is complete, true, and correct.

Petitioner's Signature

6.a. Petitioner's Signature (sign in ink)

6.b. Date of Signature (mm/dd/yyyy) 4-4-19

NOTE TO ALL PETITIONERS: If you do not completely fill out this petition or fail to submit required documents listed in the Instructions, USCIS may deny your petition.

Part 7. Interpreter's Contact Information, Certification, and Signature

Provide the following information about the interpreter if you used one.

Interpreter's Full Name

1.a. Interpreter's Family Name (Last Name)

1.b. Interpreter's Given Name (First Name)

2. Interpreter's Business or Organization Name (if any)

Interpreter's Mailing Address

3.a. Street Number and Name

3.b. ☐ Apt. ☐ Ste. ☐ Flr.

3.c. City or Town

3.d. State 3.e. ZIP Code

3.f. Province

3.g. Postal Code

3.h. Country

Interpreter's Contact Information

4. Interpreter's Daytime Telephone Number

5. Interpreter's Mobile Telephone Number (if any)

6. Interpreter's Email Address (if any)

Interpreter's Certification

I certify, under penalty of perjury, that:

I am fluent in English and ______,

which is the same language provided in **Part 6., Item Number 1.b.**, and I have read to this petitioner in the identified language every question and instruction on this petition and his or her answer to every question. The petitioner informed me that he or she understands every instruction, question, and answer on the petition, including the **Petitioner's Declaration and Certification**, and has verified the accuracy of every answer.

Interpreter's Signature

7.a. Interpreter's Signature (sign in ink)

7.b. Date of Signature (mm/dd/yyyy)

Part 8. Contact Information, Declaration, and Signature of the Person Preparing this Petition, if Other Than the Petitioner

Provide the following information about the preparer.

Preparer's Full Name

1.a. Preparer's Family Name (Last Name)

Lerner

1.b. Preparer's Given Name (First Name)

Brian

2. Preparer's Business or Organization Name (if any)

Law Offices of Brian D. Lerner, APC

Preparer's Mailing Address

3.a. Street Number and Name: 3233 E. Broadway

3.b. ☐ Apt. ☐ Ste. ☐ Flr.

3.c. City or Town: Long Beach

3.d. State: CA 3.e. ZIP Code: 90803

3.f. Province

3.g. Postal Code

3.h. Country

USA

Part 8. Contact Information, Declaration, and Signature of the Person Preparing this Petition, if Other Than the Petitioner (continued)

Preparer's Contact Information

4. Preparer's Daytime Telephone Number

5. Preparer's Mobile Telephone Number (if any)

6. Preparer's Email Address (if any)

Preparer's Statement

7.a. ☐ I am not an attorney or accredited representative but have prepared this petition on behalf of the petitioner and with the petitioner's consent.

7.b. ☒ I am an attorney or accredited representative and my representation of the petitioner in this case ☒ extends ☐ does not extend beyond the preparation of this petition.

NOTE: If you are an attorney or accredited representative whose representation extends beyond preparation of this petition, you may be obliged to submit a completed Form G-28, Notice of Entry of Appearance as Attorney or Accredited Representative, with this petition.

Preparer's Certification

By my signature, I certify, under penalty of perjury, that I prepared this petition at the request of the petitioner. The petitioner then reviewed this completed petition and informed me that he or she understands all of the information contained in, and submitted with, his or her petition, including the **Petitioner's Declaration and Certification**, and that all of this information is complete, true, and correct. I completed this petition based only on information that the petitioner provided to me or authorized me to obtain or use.

Preparer's Signature

8.a. Preparer's Signature (sign in ink)

8.b. Date of Signature (mm/dd/yyyy)

Part 9. Additional Information

If you need extra space to provide any additional information within this petition, use the space below. If you need more space than what is provided, you may make copies of this page to complete and file with this petition or attach a separate sheet of paper. Type or print your name and A-Number (if any) at the top of each sheet; indicate the **Page Number**, **Part Number**, and **Item Number** to which your answer refers; and sign and date each sheet.

1.a. Family Name (Last Name) [redacted]

1.b. Given Name (First Name) [redacted]

1.c. Middle Name [redacted]

2. A-Number (if any) ▶ A-

3.a. Page Number 4 3.b. Part Number 2 3.c. Item Number 50

3.d.
Education History:
Laguna College of Art and Design
2222 Laguna Canyon Rd, Laguna Beach, CA 92651
Fall 09-2013- Spring 06-2014
Major in Fine Arts- Drawing and Painting
Minor in Sculpture

4.a. Page Number 4.b. Part Number 4.c. Item Number

4.d.

5.a. Page Number 5.b. Part Number 5.c. Item Number

5.d.

6.a. Page Number 6.b. Part Number 6.c. Item Number

6.d.

7.a. Page Number 7.b. Part Number 7.c. Item Number

7.d.

Addendum

Form: I-130 (Page 1)

Part 2. Additional Residential History:

Supplemental Information for Spouse Beneficiary

Department of Homeland Security
U.S. Citizenship and Immigration Services

USCIS
Form I-130A
OMB No. 1615-0012
Expires 07/31/2018

To be completed by an attorney or accredited representative (if any).

☒ Select this box if Form G-28 is attached.	Volag Number (if any)	Attorney State Bar Number (if applicable)	Attorney or Accredited Representative USCIS Online Account Number (if any)

► **START HERE - Type or print in black ink.**

The purpose of this form is to collect additional information for a spouse beneficiary of Form I-130, Petition for Alien Relative. If your spouse is a U.S. citizen, lawful permanent resident, or non-citizen U.S. national who is filing Form I-130 on your behalf, you must complete and sign Form I-130A, Supplemental Information for Spouse Beneficiary, and submit it with the Form I-130 filed by your spouse. If you reside overseas, you still must complete Form I-130A, but you do not need to sign the form.

Part 1. Information About You (Spouse Beneficiary)

1. Alien Registration Number (A-Number) (if any) ► A-

2. USCIS Online Account Number (if any) ►

Your Full Name

3.a. Family Name (Last Name)

3.b. Given Name (First Name)

3.c. Middle Name

Address History

Provide your physical addresses for the last five years, whether inside or outside the United States. Provide your current address first. If you need extra space to complete this section, use the space provided in **Part 7. Additional Information.**

Physical Address 1

4.a. Street Number and Name

4.b. ☒ Apt. ☐ Ste. ☐ Flr. D

4.c. City or Town

4.d. State 4.e. ZIP Code

4.f. Province Bedfordshire

4.g. Postal Code

4.h. Country

5.a. Date From (mm/dd/yyyy) 01/13/2018

5.b. Date To (mm/dd/yyyy) PRESENT

Physical Address 2

6.a. Street Number and Name

6.b. ☐ Apt. ☐ Ste. ☐ Flr.

6.c. City or Town

6.d. State 6.e. ZIP Code

6.f. Province

6.g. Postal Code

6.h. Country United Kingdom

7.a. Date From (mm/dd/yyyy) 08/28/2008

7.b. Date To (mm/dd/yyyy) 01/12/2018

Last Physical Address Outside the United States

Provide your last address outside the United States of more than one year (even if listed above).

8.a. Street Number and Name

8.b. ☒ Apt. ☐ Ste. ☐ Flr. D

8.c. City or Town

8.d. Province

8.e. Postal Code

8.f. Country

Part 1. Information About You (The Spouse Beneficiary)

9.a. Date From (mm/dd/yyyy) 01/13/2018

9.b. Date To (mm/dd/yyyy) PRESENT

Information About Parent 1

Full Name of Parent 1

10.a. Family Name (Maiden Name) [redacted]

10.b. Given Name (First Name) [redacted]

10.c. Middle Name [redacted]

11. Date of Birth (mm/dd/yyyy) 09/20/1954

12. Sex ☐ Male ☒ Female

13. City/Town/Village of Birth [redacted]

14. Country of Birth [redacted]

15. City/Town/Village of Residence [redacted]

16. Country of Residence [redacted]

Information About Parent 2

Full Name of Parent 2

17.a. Family Name (Last Name) [redacted]

17.b. Given Name (First Name) [redacted]

17.c. Middle Name [redacted]

18. Date of Birth (mm/dd/yyyy) 05/07/1954

19. Sex ☒ Male ☐ Female

20. City/Town/Village of Birth [redacted]

21. Country of Birth [redacted]

22. City/Town/Village of Residence [redacted]

23. Country of Residence [redacted]

Part 2. Information About Your Employment

Provide your employment history for the last five years, whether inside or outside the United States. Provide your current employment first. If you are currently unemployed, type or print "Unemployed" in **Item Number 1.** below. If you need extra space to complete this section, use the space provided in **Part 7. Additional Information.**

Employment History

Employer 1

1. Name of Employer/Company RJC Projects Engineering LTD

2.a. Street Number and Name Unit 1-2 Federal Estate, Newton Road

2.b. ☐ Apt. ☐ Ste. ☐ Flr.

2.c. City or Town Rushden

2.d. State 2.e. ZIP Code

2.f. Province [redacted]

2.g. Postal Code [redacted]

2.h. Country [redacted]

3. Your Occupation Rigger/Engineer

4.a. Date From (mm/dd/yyyy) 08/01/2008

4.b. Date To (mm/dd/yyyy) PRESENT

Employer 2

5. Name of Employer/Company

6.a. Street Number and Name

6.b. ☐ Apt. ☐ Ste. ☐ Flr.

6.c. City or Town

6.d. State 6.e. ZIP Code

6.f. Province

6.g. Postal Code

6.h. Country

Part 2. Information About Your Employment (continued)

7. Your Occupation

8.a. Date From (mm/dd/yyyy)

8.b. Date To (mm/dd/yyyy)

Part 3. Information About Your Employment Outside the United States

Provide your last occupation outside the United States if not shown above. If you never worked outside the United States, provide this information in the space provided in **Part 7. Additional Information.**

1. Name of Employer/Company

2.a. Street Number and Name

2.b. ☐ Apt. ☐ Ste. ☐ Flr.

2.c. City or Town

2.d. State 2.e. ZIP Code

2.f. Province

2.g. Postal Code

2.h. Country

3. Your Occupation

4.a. Date From (mm/dd/yyyy)

4.b. Date To (mm/dd/yyyy)

Part 4. Spouse Beneficiary's Statement, Contact Information, Certification, and Signature

NOTE: Read the **Penalties** section of the Form I-130 and Form I-130A Instructions before completing this part.

Spouse Beneficiary's Statement

NOTE: Select the box for either **Item Number 1.a.** or **1.b.** If applicable, select the box for **Item Number 2.**

1.a. ☒ I can read and understand English, and I have read and understand every question and instruction on this form and my answer to every question.

1.b. ☐ The interpreter named in **Part 5.** read to me every question and instruction on this form and my answer to every question in ____, a language in which I am fluent, and I understood everything.

2. ☒ At my request, the preparer name in **Part 6.**, Bri anD. Lerner, prepared this form for me based only upon information I provided or authorized.

Spouse Beneficiary's Contact Information

3. Spouse Beneficiary's Daytime Telephone Number

4. Spouse Beneficiary's Mobile Telephone Number (if any)

5. Spouse Beneficiary's Email Address (if any)

Spouse Beneficiary's Certification

Copies of any documents I have submitted are exact photocopies of unaltered, original documents, and I understand that USCIS may require that I submit original documents to USCIS at a later date. Furthermore, I authorize the release of any information from any of my records that USCIS may need to determine my eligibility for the immigration benefit I seek.

I further authorize release of information contained in this form, in supporting documents, and in my USCIS records to other entities and persons where necessary for the administration and enforcement of U.S. immigration laws.

I certify, under penalty of perjury, that I provided or authorized all of the information in this form, I understand all of the information contained in, and submitted with, my form, and that all of this information is complete, true, and correct.

Spouse Beneficiary's Signature

6.a. Spouse Beneficiary's Signature

6.b. Date of Signature (mm/dd/yyyy) 03/29/2019

NOTE TO ALL SPOUSE BENEFICIARIES: If you do not completely fill out this form or fail to submit required documents listed in the Instructions, USCIS may deny the Form I-130 filed on your behalf.

Part 5. Interpreter's Contact Information, Certification, and Signature

Provide the following information about the interpreter you used to complete Form I-130A if he or she is different from the interpreter used to complete the Form I-130 filed on your behalf.

Interpreter's Full Name

1.a. Interpreter's Family Name (Last Name)

1.b. Interpreter's Given Name (First Name)

2. Interpreter's Business or Organization Name (if any)

Interpreter's Mailing Address

3.a. Street Number and Name

3.b. ☐ Apt. ☐ Ste. ☐ Flr.

3.c. City or Town

3.d. State 3.e. ZIP Code

3.f. Province

3.g. Postal Code

3.h. Country

Interpreter's Contact Information

4. Interpreter's Daytime Telephone Number

5. Interpreter's Mobile Telephone Number (if any)

6. Interpreter's Email Address (if any)

Interpreter's Certification

I certify, under penalty of perjury, that:

I am fluent in English and ________,

which is the same language provided in **Part 4., Item Number 1.b.**, and I have read to this spouse beneficiary in the identified language every question and instruction on this form and his or her answer to every question. The spouse beneficiary informed me that he or she understands every instruction, question, and answer on the form, including the **Spouse Beneficiary's Certification**, and has verified the accuracy of every answer.

Interpreter's Signature

7.a. Interpreter's Signature

7.b. Date of Signature (mm/dd/yyyy)

Part 6. Contact Information, Declaration, and Signature of the Person Preparing this Form, if Other Than the Spouse Beneficiary

Provide the following information about the preparer you used to complete Form I-130A if he or she is different from the preparer used to complete the Form I-130 filed on your behalf.

Preparer's Full Name

1.a. Preparer's Family Name (Last Name)
Lerner

1.b. Preparer's Given Name (First Name)
Brian

2. Preparer's Business or Organization Name (if any)
Law Offices of Brian D. Lerner, APC

Preparer's Mailing Address

3.a. Street Number and Name: 3233 E. Broadway

3.b. ☐ Apt. ☐ Ste. ☐ Flr.

3.c. City or Town: Long Beach

3.d. State: CA 3.e. ZIP Code: 90803

3.f. Province

3.g. Postal Code

3.h. Country
USA

Part 6. Contact Information, Declaration, and Signature of the Person Preparing this Form, if Other Than the Spouse Beneficiary (continued)

Preparer's Contact Information

4. Preparer's Daytime Telephone Number

(562) 495-0554

5. Preparer's Mobile Telephone Number (if any)

6. Preparer's Email Address (if any)

blerner@californiaimmigration.us

Preparer's Statement

7.a. ☐ I am not an attorney or accredited representative but have prepared this form on behalf of the spouse beneficiary and with the spouse beneficiary's consent.

7.b. ☒ I am an attorney or accredited representative and my representation of the spouse beneficiary in this case ☒ extends ☐ does not extend beyond the preparation of this form.

NOTE: If you are an attorney or accredited representative whose representation extends beyond preparation of this form, you may be obliged to submit a completed Form G-28, Notice of Entry of Appearance as Attorney or Accredited Representative, with this form.

Preparer's Certification

By my signature, I certify, under penalty of perjury, that I prepared this form at the request of the spouse beneficiary. The spouse beneficiary then reviewed this completed form and informed me that he or she understands all of the information contained in, and submitted with, his or her form, including the **Spouse Beneficiary's Certification**, and that all of this information is complete, true, and correct. I completed this form based only on information that the spouse beneficiary provided to me or authorized me to obtain or use.

Preparer's Signature

8.a. Preparer's Signature

8.b. Date of Signature (mm/dd/yyyy)

Part 7. Additional Information

If you need extra space to provide any additional information within this form, use the space below. If you need more space than what is provided, you may make copies of this page to complete and file with this form or attach a separate sheet of paper. Type or print your name and A-Number (if any) at the top of each sheet; indicate the **Page Number**, **Part Number**, and **Item Number** to which your answer refers; and sign and date each sheet.

1.a. Family Name (Last Name) [redacted]

1.b. Given Name (First Name) [redacted]

1.c. Middle Name [redacted]

2. A-Number (if any) ▶ A-

3.a. Page Number 3.b. Part Number 3.c. Item Number

3.d.

4.a. Page Number 4.b. Part Number 4.c. Item Number

4.d.

5.a. Page Number 5.b. Part Number 5.c. Item Number

5.d.

6.a. Page Number 6.b. Part Number 6.c. Item Number

6.d.

7.a. Page Number 7.b. Part Number 7.c. Item Number

7.d.

EXHIBITS

EXHIBIT '1':

Petitioner's Birth Certificate

STATE OF CALIFORNIA

CERTIFICATION OF VITAL RECORD

COUNTY OF LOS ANGELES

REGISTRAR-RECORDER/COUNTY CLERK

104- STATE FILE NUMBER

CERTIFICATE OF LIVE BIRTH
STATE OF CALIFORNIA
USE BLACK INK ONLY

J90 9085790
LOCAL REGISTRATION DISTRICT AND CERTIFICATE NUMBER

THIS CHILD	1A. NAME OF CHILD—FIRST (GIVEN): [redacted]	1B. MIDDLE: [redacted]	1C. LAST (FAMILY): [redacted]		
	2. SEX: FEMALE	3A. THIS BIRTH SINGLE, TWIN, ETC.: SINGLE	3B. IF MULTIPLE, THIS CHILD 1ST, 2ND, ETC.: -	4A. DATE OF BIRTH—MONTH, DAY, YEAR: MAY 21, 1990	4B. HOUR—(24 HOUR CLOCK TIME): [redacted]
PLACE OF BIRTH	5A. PLACE OF BIRTH—NAME OF HOSPITAL OR FACILITY: [redacted]	5B. STREET ADDRESS—STREET, NUMBER, OR LOCATION: [redacted]			
	5C. CITY: [redacted]	5D. COUNTY: [redacted]	5E. PLANNED PLACE OF BIRTH: HOSPITAL		
FATHER OF CHILD	6A. NAME OF FATHER—FIRST (GIVEN): [redacted]	6B. MIDDLE: [redacted]	6C. LAST (FAMILY): [redacted]	7. STATE OF BIRTH: CA	8. DATE OF BIRTH: 1/5/65
MOTHER OF CHILD	9A. NAME OF MOTHER—FIRST (GIVEN): [redacted]	9B. MIDDLE: [redacted]	9C. LAST (MAIDEN): [redacted]	10. STATE OF BIRTH: CA	11. DATE OF BIRTH: 12/27/65
PARENT'S CERTIFICATION	I CERTIFY THAT I HAVE REVIEWED THE STATED INFORMATION AND THAT IT IS TRUE AND CORRECT TO THE BEST OF MY KNOWLEDGE	12A. PARENT OR OTHER INFORMANT—SIGNATURE: [redacted]	12B. RELATIONSHIP TO CHILD: Birth Clerk	12C. DATE SIGNED: 7-6-90	
CERTIFICATION OF BIRTH	I CERTIFY THAT THE CHILD WAS BORN ALIVE AT THE DATE, HOUR AND PLACE STATED	13A. ATTENDANT OR CERTIFIER—SIGNATURE—DEGREE OR TITLE: [redacted]	13B. LICENSE NUMBER: C09697	13C. DATE SIGNED: 7-4-90	
	13D. TYPED NAME, TITLE AND MAILING ADDRESS OF ATTENDANT: [redacted]	14. TYPED NAME AND TITLE OF CERTIFIER IF OTHER THAN ATTENDANT			
LOCAL REGISTRAR	15A. DATE OF DEATH	15B. STATE FILE NO. (STATE USE ONLY)	16. LOCAL REGISTRAR: [redacted]	17. DATE ACCEPTED FOR REGISTRATION: JUL 30 1990	

CALOSANG02

This is to certify that this document is a true copy of the official record filed with the Registrar-Recorder/County Clerk.

Dean C. Logan

MAR 2 9 2019

EXHIBIT '2':

Petitioner's Passport

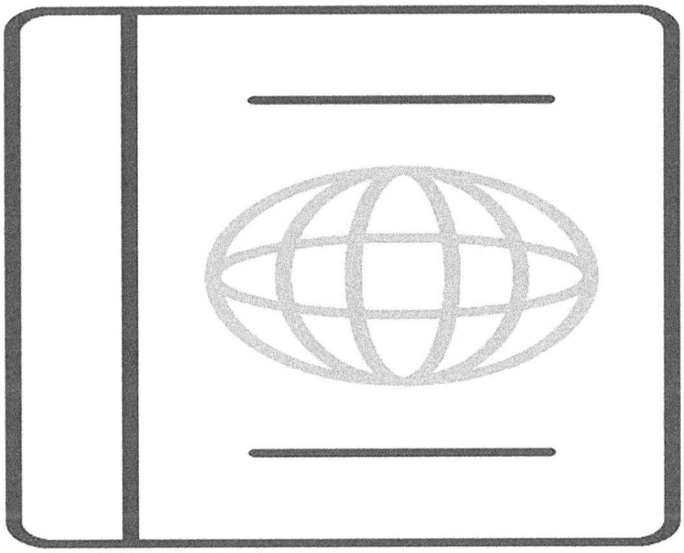

We the People
Of the United States,
in Order to form a more perfect Union,
establish Justice, insure domestic Tranquility,
provide for the common defence,
promote the general Welfare, and secure
the Blessings of Liberty to ourselves and
our Posterity, do ordain and establish this
Constitution for the United States of America.
SIGNATURE OF BEARER / SIGNATURE DU TITULAIRE / FIRMA DEL TITULAR
PASSPORT
PASSEPORT
PASAPORTE
UNITED STATES OF AMERICA
USA
P
USA
UNITED STATES OF AMERICA
CALIFORNIA, U.S.A.
F
24 Oct 2014
United States
Department of State
23 Oct 2024
SEE PAGE 27
USA

EXHIBIT '3':

Beneficiary's Birth Certificate

CAUTION [illegible] y person who (1) falsifies any of the parti[illegible] on this certificate or (2) uses a falsified c[illegible] cate as true knowing it to be false, is liable to prosecution.

CERTIFIED COPY OF AN ENTRY

Pursuant to the Births and Deaths Registration Act 1953

NHS Number GKASS 108 — BIRTH — Entry No. 108

Registration district

Sub-district

Administrative area

	CHILD	
1. Date and place of birth	Twelfth July 1982.	
2. Name and surname		3. Sex: Male

	FATHER
4. Name and surname	Michael Andrew
5. Place of birth	Germany
6. Occupation	Foreman/Diesel fitter

	MOTHER	
7. Name and surname		
8. Place of birth	Newport Pagnell, Bucks.	
9. (a) Maiden surname		(b) Surname at marriage if different from maiden surname: ---
10. Usual address (if different from place of child's birth)	12, Belvoir Walk, Bedford.	

INFORMANT	
11. Name and surname (if not the mother or father): ---	12. Qualification: Mother
13. Usual address (if different from that in 10 above): ---	
14. I certify that the particulars entered above are true to the best of my knowledge and belief: J.	Signature of informant
15. Date of registration: Fourteenth July 1982.	16. Signature of registrar:
17. *Name given after registration, and surname: ---	

* See note overleaf

Certified to be a true copy of an entry in a register in my custody

R. [illegible] Registrar — 14th July 1982. Date

B. Cert.
R B D

EXHIBIT '4':

Beneficiary's Passport and Visa

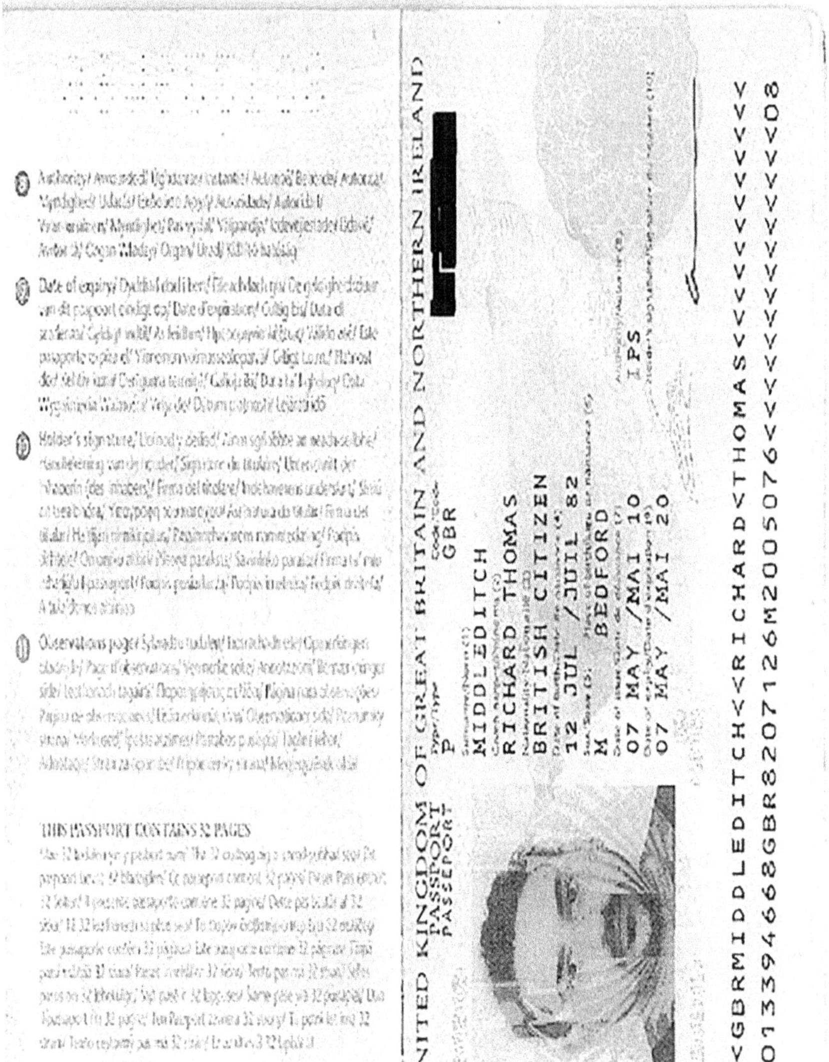
UNITED KINGDOM OF GREAT BRITAIN AND NORTHERN IRELAND
PASSPORT
PASSEPORT
P
GBR
MIDDLEDITCH
RICHARD THOMAS
BRITISH CITIZEN
12 JUL /JUIL 82
M
BEDFORD
07 MAY /MAI 10
IPS
07 MAY /MAI 20
THIS PASSPORT CONTAINS 32 PAGES
P<GBRMIDDLEDITCH<<RICHARD<THOMAS<<<<<<<<<<<<
8013394668GBR8207126M2005076<<<<<<<<<<<<<<08

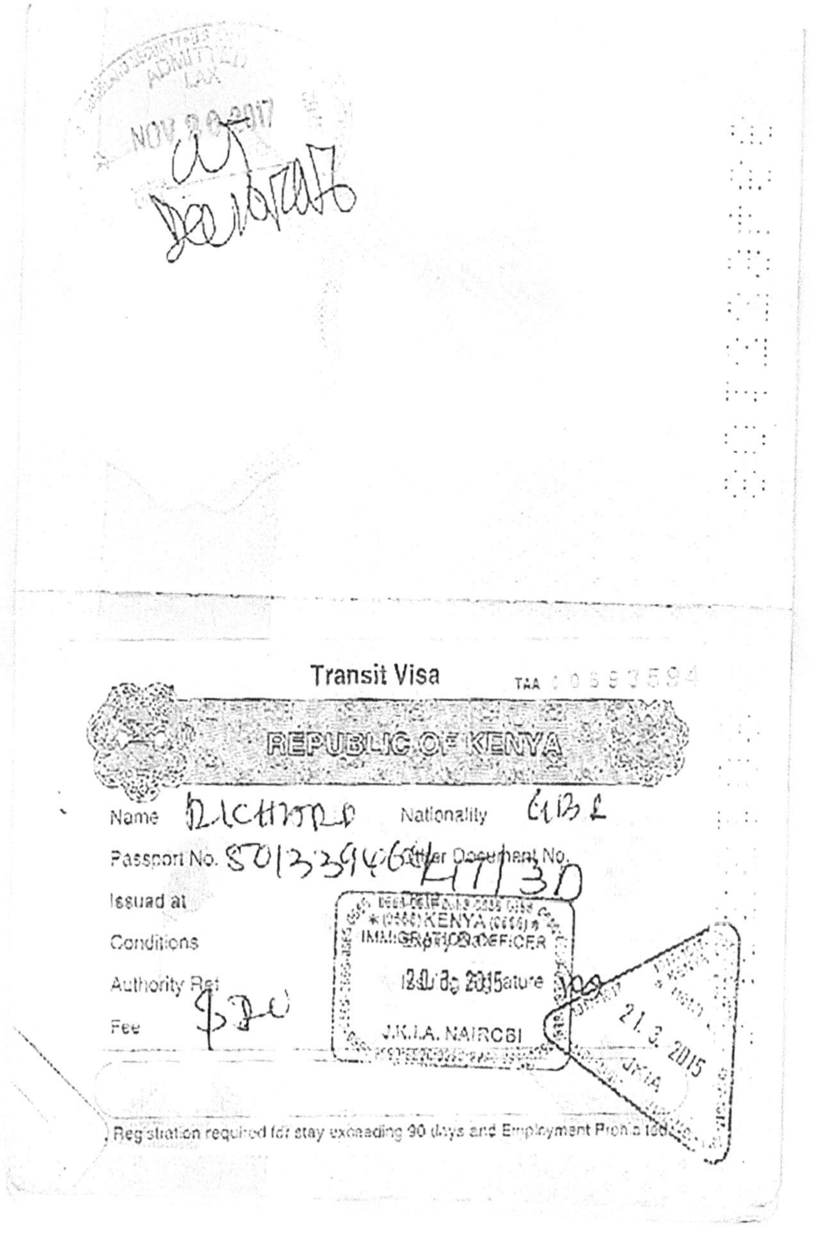
ADMITTED
LAX
Transit Visa
REPUBLIC OF KENYA
Name
Nationality
Passport No.
Other Document No.
Issued at
Conditions
Authority Ref
Fee
KENYA
IMMIGRATION OFFICER
J.K.I.A. NAIROBI
21. 3. 2015
JKIA

Passport Number : **801339466**

Passport Country of Issuance : **United Kingdom**

	Date	Type	Location
1	2019-01-02	Departure	LOS
2	2018-12-26	Arrival	LOS
3	2018-05-26	Departure	LOS
4	2018-05-19	Arrival	LOS
5	2018-02-25	Departure	Unavailable
6	2018-02-15	Arrival	LOS
7	2017-11-27	Departure	Unavailable
8	2017-11-20	Arrival	LOS
9	2016-04-25	Departure	LOS
10	2016-04-15	Arrival	LOS

EXHIBIT '5':

Petitioner and Beneficiary's Marriage Certificate

Printed by authority of the Registrar General

TN 388489

CERTIFIED COPY OF AN ENTRY OF MARRIAGE
Pursuant to the Marriage Act 1949

M. Cert.
S.R./R.B.D.&M.

Registration District Milton Keynes

2019. Marriage solemnized at Flowers Suite Civic Offices 1 Saxon Gate East Milton Keynes in the District of Milton Keynes in the Borough of Milton Keynes

Columns:— 1		2	3	4	5	6	7	8
No.	When married	Name and surname	Age	Condition	Rank or profession	Residence at the time of marriage	Father's name and surname	Rank or profession of father
75	1st February	H	years	Single	Engineer	Flat 37 Kimbolton Rd Bc	Michael Andrews MIDDLEDITCH	M
						PB		

Married in the Flowers Suite by Certificate before me.

This marriage was solemnized between us, | in the presence of us, M R | D J Dachtler Deputy Superintendent Registar; J Radford Deputy Registrar

Deputy

3188496

ENDORSED - FILED
In the office of the Secretary of State
of the State of California

FEB 13 2009

ARTICLES OF INCORPORATION

ARTICLE I

The name of this corporation is [redacted] Inc.

ARTICLE II

The purpose of this corporation is to engage in any lawful act or activity for which a corporation [redacted] be organized under the General Corporation Law of California other han the banking business, the trust company business or the practice of a profession permitted to be incorporated by the California Corporations Code.

ARTICLE III

The name and address in the State of California of this corporation's initial agent for service of process is:

ARTICLE IV

This corporation is authorized to issue only one class of shares of stock; and the total number of shares which the corporation is authorized to issue is one million (1,000,000).

ARTICLE V

The liability of directors of the corporation for monetary damages shall be eliminated to the fullest extent permissible under California law. The corporation is authorized to provide indemnification of agents (as defined in Section 317 of the California Corporations Code) through Bylaw provisions, agreements with agents, vote of shareholders or disinterested directors, or otherwise, to the fullest extent permissible under California law. Any amendment, repeal or modification of this provision of this Article V shall not adversely affect any right or protection of an agent of this corporation existing at the time of such amendment, repeal or modification.

Dated: February 12, 2009

[redacted] Incorporator

OFFICE OF THE

Our Wedding

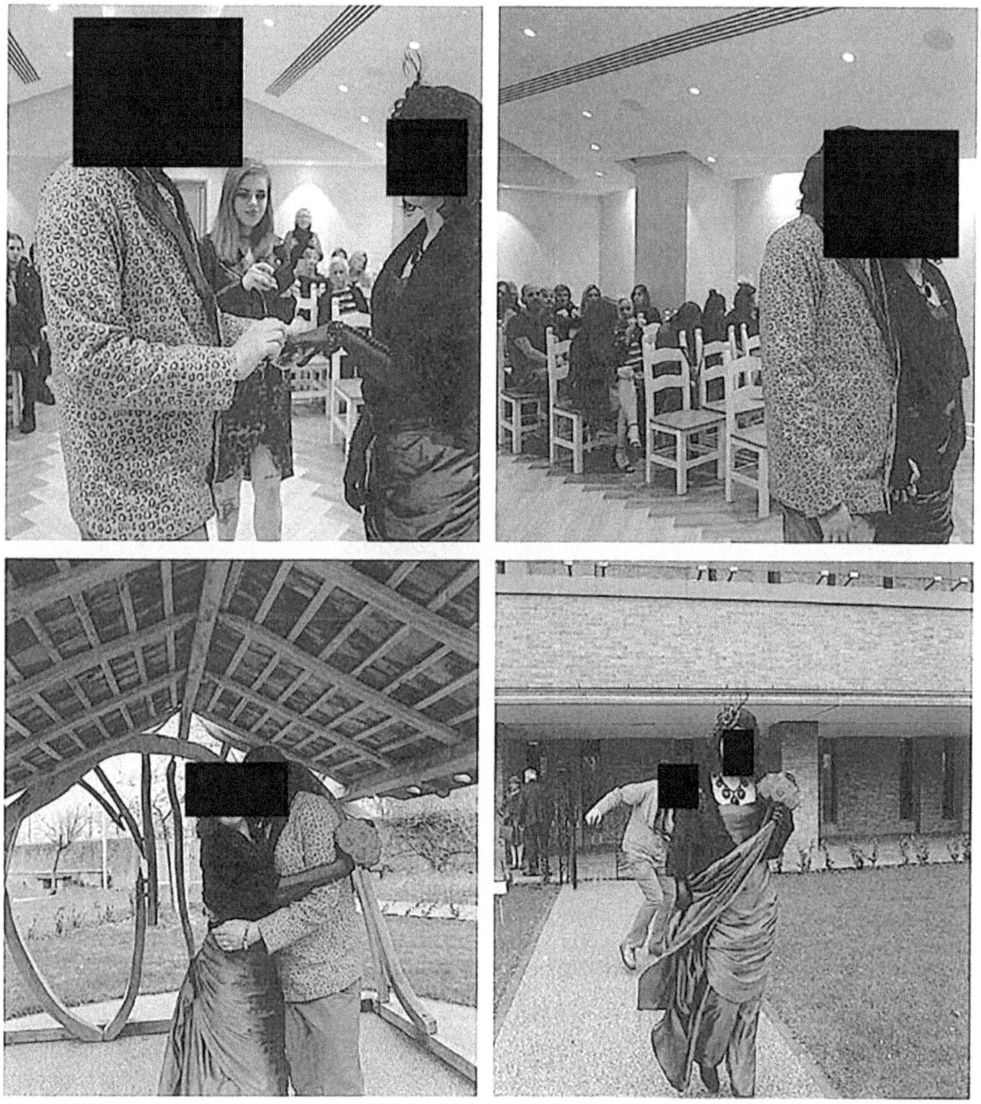

Our Wedding

EXHIBIT '7':

Supporting Letters from the Relatives and Friends of Petitioner and Beneficiary

26th March 2019

Jo-Anne Marie

OF SUPPPORT FOR AND

To whom it may concern

My name is Jo-Anne Marie and I was born on 20th September 1954 in the town of Newport Pagnell, Bucks, England. I am mother and have known since they began dating a few years ago. Since then my husband and I have met on several occasions when she has visited the UK to be with and that has been to see in California as many times as holiday allowances will permit. We have also met parents and some of her extended family.

and got engaged last September and then proceeded to go through the rather complicated process (as she is not a UK resident) of getting married in the UK. Whilst engaged, they went on a course and each made the others wedding rings. Their wedding was a happy and joyous occasion attended by both of their families and friends and they are both saving hard to build up a deposit for their first home together.

It is my opinion that and are in love and committed to each other. I believe they have made a lifetime commitment to each other and are happy. I appreciated the opportunity to provide this information. Should you have any questions or need more information, my contact numbers are:-

Yours sincerely

Jo-Anne

Kimberly

March 27, 2019

Subject: Letter of Support for &

To Whom It May Concern:

My name is Kimberly and I was born on 27 December 1965 in Los Angeles, California.

I am the mother of and have known since December of 2014 when they met.

Since that time, my husband, Tom, who is father, have had the privilege to get to know and feel he is a very stand-up and respectable man who loves our daughter unconditionally. Also, we have witnessed on many occasions and family get togethers, their sincere love and devotion for each other.

It is without a doubt in our opinion that and are truly in love. The love, devotion and respect that they have for each other is transparent in their actions. They are obviously overly joyed at being married and take very seriously their marriage vows they have sworn to uphold and the commitment that comes with those vows.

I am very appreciative to share my thoughts and feelings of this very happy and loving couple.

Should you need further information from me, please contact me at .

Sincerely yours,

Kimberly

4/5/2019

Ramsey Roberts
█████████████
███████████████

Subject: Letter of Support for █████ Morgan and █████ Middleditch.

To Whom It May Concern:

My name is Ramsey Roberts. I was born on March 20, 1981 in Cincinnati, Ohio. I moved to Long Beach, California 11 years ago on June 5th, and I have known Courtney █████ for over 5 of those years. I've known █████ ██████ for over a year. █████ and I met for the first time around Thanksgiving in Long Beach on one of his visits to see Courtney. Since then I have gotten to know him during his visits to the U.S., on quiet nights in as well as when he has joined us out for karaoke.

Last August I went to a music festival with Courtney, █████ and our mutual friend Brandon in Blackpool, England. We (█████ █████ and I) first met up in London shortly after I arrived, and he was more than happy to show us around. █████ is a great host and we all had a nice time.

Most recently I flew out to England to attend their wedding in Milton Keynes and was asked to be a witness at the ceremony. Both █████ and Courtney's friends and family came from all over the world to celebrate their union, enjoy the ceremony and reception, and everyone had a great time.

It is my opinion that █████ and █████ are in love and committed to each other. I believe they have made a lifetime commitment to each other and are happy.

I appreciate the opportunity to provide this information. Should you have any questions or need more information, my contact number is 1 ██████

Sincerely,

Ramsey Roberts

Friday, April 5, 19

Catherine Taylor

Subject: Letter of Support for and

To Whom It May Concern:

My name is Catherine Taylor and I was born on 2nd December 1980 in Perth, Western Australia. My parents are British and we moved back to the UK in my teens, so I am a dual British/Australian citizen. I moved to Los Angeles a few years ago, as a Fulbright Scholar, to complete my Masters at the American Film Institute.

I have known since September 25th, 2004, when we both went to see a band in Islington, London. We have been very close friends ever since, we lived together for over a year, and we have been on holiday together numerous times. Over the years I have met all of girlfriends, because I know him so well, he would bring them over so I could see if they were well suited.

In all my years of knowing I have never seen him in love and committed like he is with The moment he introduced her to me I knew she was the one for him, and I could see she felt the same way. I was surprised it took them as long as it did to get married, I really thought they were going to drive down to Vegas in the first year, but I suppose, when you're going to spend the rest of your lives together, there's no need to rush the wedding.

I am delighted that and have found each other. I have no doubt that they will be together forever, and they are blissfully happy. I appreciate the opportunity to provide this information. Should you have any questions or need more information, my contact number is

8/4/2019
Matthew Doughty

Subject: Letter of Support for [redacted] & [redacted] [redacted]

To Whom It May Concern:

My name is Matthew Doughty, and I was born on 10/1/1985. I have known [redacted] since I started university in 2007. We instantly became friends, lived together as flatmates for a couple of years and have stayed in contact ever since, going out drinking or simply hanging out. I'm also known by his family as I've been there for Christmas a few times.

About a couple of years ago [redacted] was telling me about [redacted] who he met in London while she was on holiday and how amazing she was talking about her hobbies and showing me pictures. He would often disappear telling me that he's in the US meeting her. Then later say some stories about his trips. Over time I got the pleasure of talking to her over webcam myself and then eventually I got to meet her in person. They are a wonderful couple and clearly in love with each-other.

After sometime [redacted] told me they are going to get married in 2019 and I was invited to be the best man. The wedding was awesome, I got to meet 2 of [redacted] friends and of course her Mother and Father. The two families got on well together and [redacted] father gave a very emotional speech at the wedding reception.

Honestly I don't know what else I'm meant to say here, I'm very happy for them and glad that I was given the opportunity to provide this information.
Should you have any questions or need more information, my contact number is +44

Sincerely,
MDoughty
Matthew Doughty

ABOUT THE AUTHOR

Brian D. Lerner is an Immigration Lawyer and runs a National Immigration Law Firm for nearly 30 years. He is an attorney who is a certified specialist that might help in Immigration & Nationality Law as issued by the California State Bar, Board of Legal Specialization. Attorney Lerner is an expert in Immigration Law, Removal and Deportation, Citizenship, Waiver and Appeals.

He has been a licensed attorney since 1992 and started the Law Offices of Brian D. Lerner, APC. The immigration practice consists of Immigration and Nationality Law, and everything involved with and regarding immigration which includes citizenship, investment visas, family and employment visas, removal and deportation hearings, appeals, waivers, adjustment, consulate processing and all types of immigration and citizenship matters.

He has represented clients from all over the U.S. and in many countries around the world. One side of his practice is dedicated to keeping people in the U.S. and fighting for their immigration rights, while another side is to get people back who have been deported and removed from the U.S.

Also, there is the affirmative part of Immigration Law which Brian Lerner has helped numerous people come into the U.S. on business visas, investment visas, student visas, fiancée and marriage visas, religious visas and many more. Attorney Lerner has helped immigrants who are victims of crime and domestic violence or ones that are married to abusers.

In other words, Attorney Lerner has a firm that helps people all over the U.S. He has dedicated significant time to preparing numerous petitions and applications for you to get at a fraction of the price of hiring an attorney. He says it is the next best thing to a real attorney because they are real petitions prepared by an expert.

www.ingramcontent.com/pod-product-compliance
Lightning Source LLC
LaVergne TN
LVHW070911210926
848482LV00017B/1050